# THIS BOOK

Belongs to

# COLOR TEST

# 1 ONE

# REPEAT

# 2 TWO

# REPEAT

# 3 THREE

# REPEAT

# 4 FOUR

REPEAT

# 4 FOUR

# REPEAT

# 5   FIVE

# REPEAT

# 6 SIX

REPEAT

# 7 SEVEN

# REPEAT

# 8 EIGHT

# REPEAT

# 9     NINE

# REPEAT

# 10 TEN

# REPEAT

# Draw 5 candles on the cake and colour.

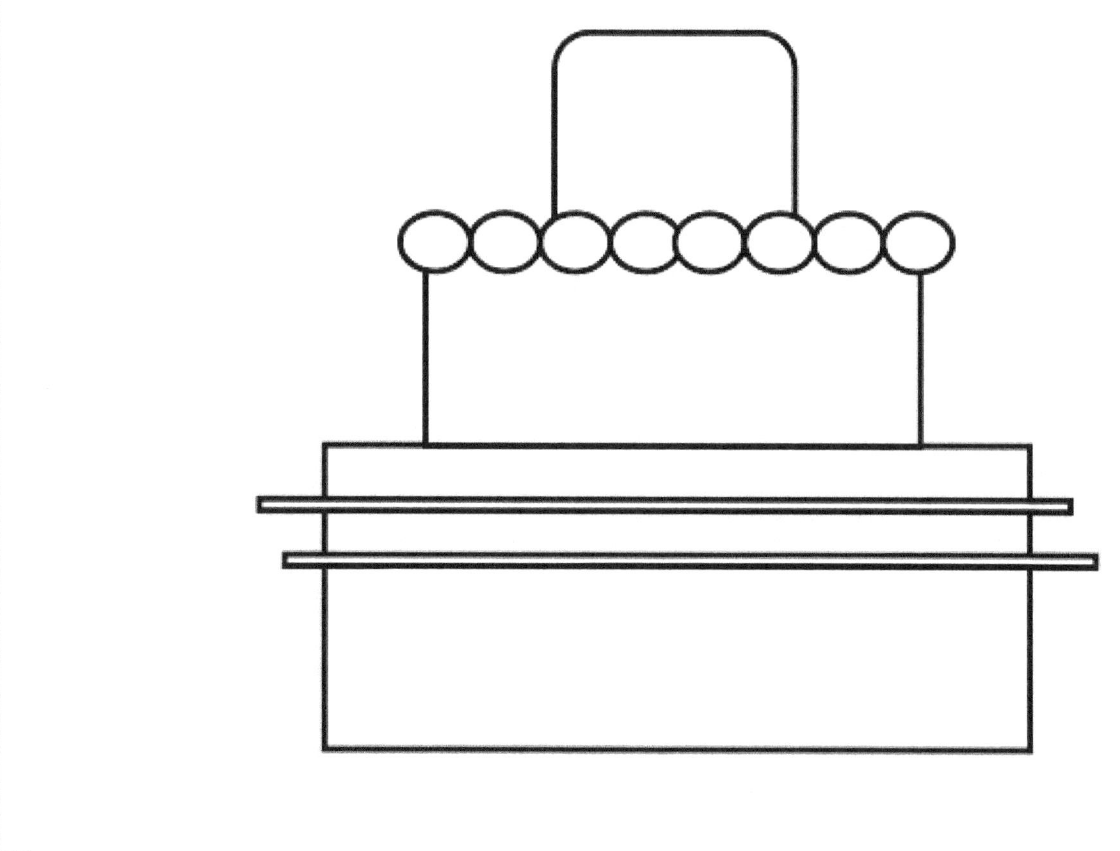

REPEAT

# Color 3 cars.

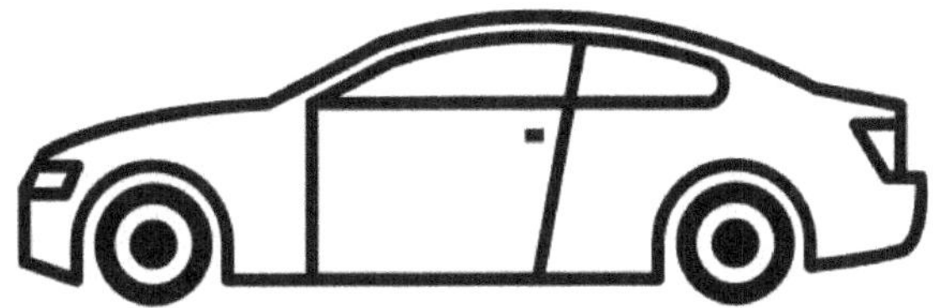

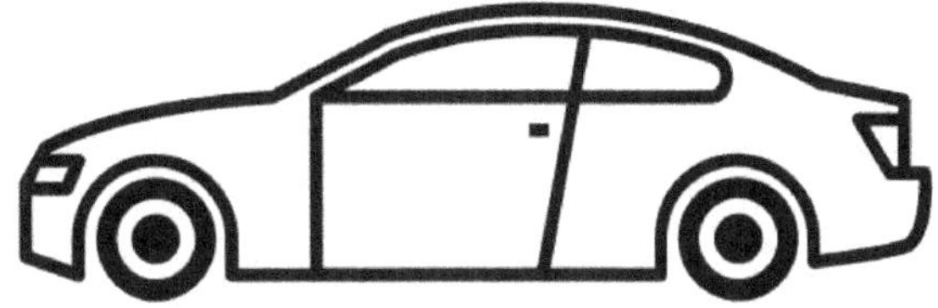

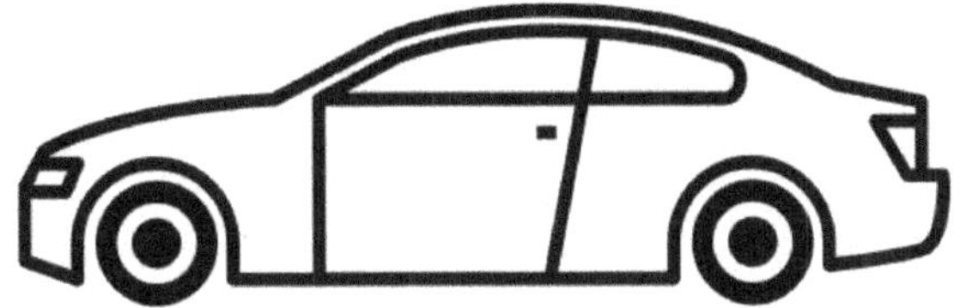

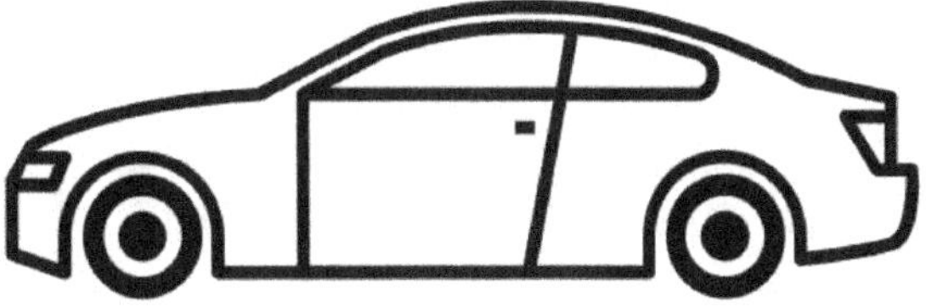

# REPEAT

# Draw 7 dots and color a ladybug.

# REPEAT

# Color 4 balloons.

# REPEAT

# Draw 1 mushroom and color the picture.

# REPEAT

# Color 3 clouds.

# REPEAT

# Draw 8 Christmas ball.

# REPEAT

# Draw 10 glitmmers for the Sun and color it.

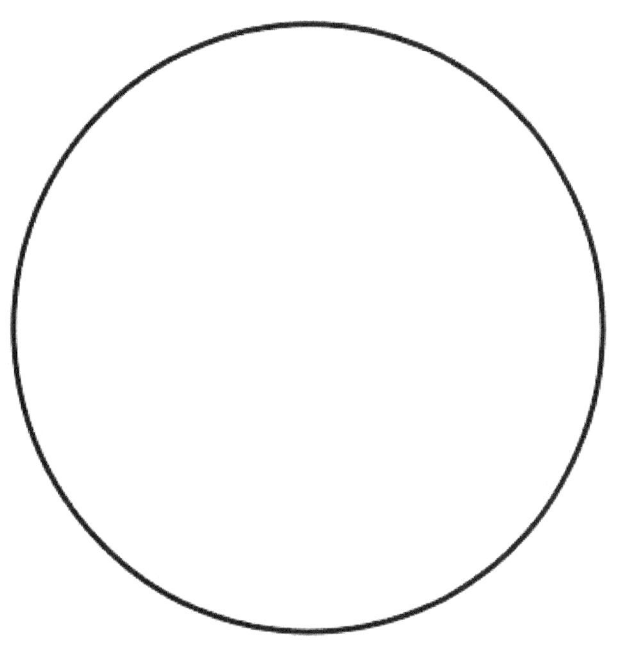

# REPEAT

# Color 2 presents.

# REPEAT

Illustrated by Vecteezy